FUN WITH
National
Parks

FUN WITH National Parks

A BIG Activity Book for Kids about America's Natural Wonders

NICOLE CLAESEN

ILLUSTRATED BY CANDELA FERRÁNDEZ

Z KIDS • NEW YORK

Zeitgeist™ is a trademark of Penguin Random House LLC ISBN:

9780593435878

Map pp. 12–13 © Samsonova Karina

Illustrations by Candela Ferrández

Author photograph © by Stephen Ironside

Illustrator photograph © by Artur Laperla

Cover design by Aimee Fleck

Book design by Erin Yeung and Aimee Fleck

Manufactured in China

2nd Printing

TO WILLIAM, ZACH, AND NATE—
YOU ARE MY WHOLE HEART!
OUR TRIPS TO NATIONAL PARKS AND
ALL THE INCREDIBLE MEMORIES MADE
ALONG THE WAY INSPIRED THIS BOOK.

Contents

☆ Denotes the ten most visited national parks

INTERMOUNTAIN REGION

PACIFIC REGION

MIDWEST REGION

ALASKA REGION

Welcome to America's Natural Wonders!

My family loves to visit national parks when we travel. Each park is unique and awe-inspiring, and we always enjoy the outdoor activities each park offers. With giant trees, deep canyons, stunning waterfalls, magnificent geysers, tall cliffs, pristine lakes, and majestic mountains, America's 63 national parks will amaze you at every turn!

So, what exactly is a national park? A national park is an area that the federal government protects for the preservation of the natural environment. A national park has historical, scientific, cultural, or environmental importance deserving of respect and care. The difference between a national park and a state or local park is that national parks are usually much bigger in size, and the federal government owns them. Many of America's national parks are on land that belonged to Native American tribes; the parks are beginning to acknowledge this history with monuments, artifacts, and other ways to preserve important Native American spaces and contributions.

America's 63 national parks are spread throughout the United States and two US territories. In this book, the parks are divided into regions determined by the National Park Service, and then listed alphabetically by state within that region. (For example, you'll find Biscayne National Park listed as the first national park in Florida in the Southeast Region.) This way, you'll be able to see where each of the parks is located and which are close to each other in case you're planning a national parks road trip. As you go through the book, you'll see a star next to the 10 most visited national parks. Be sure to put a star next to the parks you want to visit!

As you turn the pages, you'll learn which national park is located on a supervolcano, which park protects America's tallest sand dune, which park recorded a temperature of 134 degrees Fahrenheit (that's hot!), which park has the largest living tree, and so much more! You'll also get to do word searches, spot the difference, code breakers, matching, and other activities—plus you'll learn amazing facts about our incredible, diverse national parks.

Whether you love nature, activities, or weird facts, you'll find lots to enjoy in this book. So pick up a pencil, open your mind, and have fun on your journey through our glorious national parks!

America's National Parks

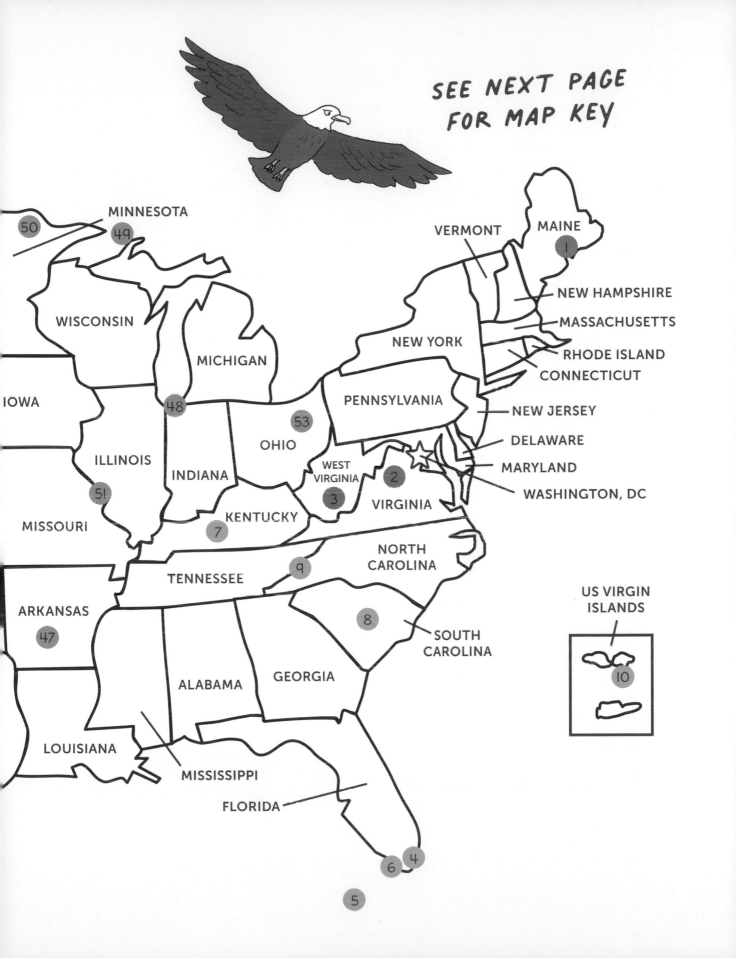

SEE NEXT PAGE FOR MAP KEY

Map Key

1. *ACADIA NATIONAL PARK (ME)

2. SHENANDOAH NATIONAL PARK (VA)

3. NEW RIVER GORGE NATIONAL PARK & PRESERVE (WV)

4. BISCAYNE NATIONAL PARK (FL)

5. DRY TORTUGAS NATIONAL PARK (FL)

6. EVERGLADES NATIONAL PARK (FL)

7. MAMMOTH CAVE NATIONAL PARK (KY)

8. CONGAREE NATIONAL PARK (SC)

9. *GREAT SMOKY MOUNTAINS NATIONAL PARK (TN/NC)

10. VIRGIN ISLANDS NATIONAL PARK (VI)

11. *GRAND CANYON NATIONAL PARK (AZ)

12. PETRIFIED FOREST NATIONAL PARK (AZ)

13. SAGUARO NATIONAL PARK (AZ)

14. BLACK CANYON OF THE GUNNISON NATIONAL PARK (CO)

15. GREAT SAND DUNES NATIONAL PARK & PRESERVE (CO)

16. MESA VERDE NATIONAL PARK (CO)

17. *ROCKY MOUNTAIN NATIONAL PARK (CO)

18. GLACIER NATIONAL PARK (MT)

19. CARLSBAD CAVERNS NATIONAL PARK (NM)

20. WHITE SANDS NATIONAL PARK (NM)

21. BIG BEND NATIONAL PARK (TX)

22. GUADALUPE MOUNTAINS NATIONAL PARK (TX)

23. ARCHES NATIONAL PARK (UT)

24. BRYCE CANYON NATIONAL PARK (UT)

25. CANYONLANDS NATIONAL PARK (UT)

26. CAPITOL REEF NATIONAL PARK (UT)

27. *ZION NATIONAL PARK (UT)

28. *GRAND TETON NATIONAL PARK (WY)

29. *YELLOWSTONE NATIONAL PARK (WY)

30 NATIONAL PARK OF AMERICAN SAMOA (AS)

31 CHANNEL ISLANDS NATIONAL PARK (CA)

32 DEATH VALLEY NATIONAL PARK (CA)

33 *JOSHUA TREE NATIONAL PARK (CA)

34 KINGS CANYON NATIONAL PARK (CA)

35 LASSEN VOLCANIC NATIONAL PARK (CA)

36 PINNACLES NATIONAL PARK (CA)

37 REDWOOD NATIONAL PARK (CA)

38 SEQUOIA NATIONAL PARK (CA)

39 YOSEMITE NATIONAL PARK (CA)

40 HALEAKALA NATIONAL PARK (HI)

41 HAWAI'I VOLCANOES NATIONAL PARK (HI)

42 GREAT BASIN NATIONAL PARK (NV)

43 CRATER LAKE NATIONAL PARK (OR)

44 MOUNT RAINIER NATIONAL PARK (WA)

45 NORTH CASCADES NATIONAL PARK (WA)

46 *OLYMPIC NATIONAL PARK (WA)

47 HOT SPRINGS NATIONAL PARK (AR)

48 INDIANA DUNES NATIONAL PARK (IN)

49 ISLE ROYALE NATIONAL PARK (MI)

50 VOYAGEURS NATIONAL PARK (MN)

51 GATEWAY ARCH NATIONAL PARK (MO)

52 THEODORE ROOSEVELT NATIONAL PARK (ND)

53 *CUYAHOGA VALLEY NATIONAL PARK (OH)

54 BADLANDS NATIONAL PARK (SD)

55 WIND CAVE NATIONAL PARK (SD)

56 DENALI NATIONAL PARK & PRESERVE (AK)

57 GATES OF THE ARCTIC NATIONAL PARK & PRESERVE (AK)

58 GLACIER BAY NATIONAL PARK & PRESERVE (AK)

59 KATMAI NATIONAL PARK & PRESERVE (AK)

60 KENAI FJORDS NATIONAL PARK (AK)

61 KOBUK VALLEY NATIONAL PARK (AK)

62 LAKE CLARK NATIONAL PARK & PRESERVE (AK)

63 WRANGELL-ST. ELIAS NATIONAL PARK & PRESERVE (AK)

Northeast & Capital Region

The Northeast and Capital Region is made up of Connecticut, Delaware, Maine, Maryland, Massachusetts, New Hampshire, New Jersey, New York, Pennsylvania, Rhode Island, Vermont, Virginia, and West Virginia. This US region is the smallest in size but is big on history and beautiful fall foliage. Because of the smaller land area, you can visit many parks in different states in a short amount of time. Nature is at its finest with large forests, deep gorges, beautiful birds, and rocky shorelines. The climates are also varied: the average January high temperature in Augusta, Maine, is 25 to 30 degrees Fahrenheit while the average January high temperature in Richmond, Virginia, is 45 to 50 degrees Fahrenheit.

☆Acadia National Park

Acadia National Park was the first national park east of the Mississippi River. It was named Sieur de Monts National Monument in 1916, then Lafayette National Park in 1919, and then Acadia National Park in 1929. There are more than 20 summits and mountains inside the park, including Cadillac Mountain (which is 1,530 feet tall), over 1,000 plant species, and hundreds of birds, including owls and bald eagles. Visitors can even go whale watching in the summer to see humpback whales that sometimes leap right out of the water!

CAN YOU CRACK THE CODE?

Four tribes, collectively known as the Wabanaki, live throughout Maine, and Acadia lies in the Wabanaki homeland. Can you use the code to discover what Wabanaki means?

22	19	12	22	6	19		12	23

26	13	19		21	4	8	18	6	4	18	21

KEY

1	2	3	4	5	6	7	8	9	10	11	12	13
R	G	I	A	M	L	U	W	B	K	V	O	H

14	15	16	17	18	19	20	21	22	23	24	25	26
Q	Z	C	J	N	E	X	D	P	F	S	Y	T

THE BALD EAGLE, WHICH YOU CAN FIND IN ACADIA NATIONAL PARK, IS THE NATIONAL BIRD OF THE UNITED STATES. HERE'S HOW TO DRAW ONE.

NOW DRAW ONE ON YOUR OWN!

Shenandoah National Park

Shenandoah National Park has rocks that are over one billion years old! It is also the only place in the world where you can find the endangered Shenandoah salamander. In 1929, President Herbert Hoover bought land (in what later became the park) called Rapidan Camp and built a cabin known as the Brown House, where he enjoyed time away from the White House. It still stands today. There are many waterfalls in the park, including the 93-foot-tall Overall Run Falls. Skyline Drive is the only public road through the park; driving the entire length takes about three hours.

YOU CAN MAKE MORE THAN 2,000 WORDS FROM THE LETTERS IN SHENANDOAH SALAMANDER. LIST EIGHT NEW WORDS HERE. (EXAMPLE: DREAM)

1. _____

2. _____

3. _____

4. _____

5. _____

6. _____

7. _____

8. _____

CIRCLE THE SIX DIFFERENCES BETWEEN THESE TWO PICTURES OF RAPIDAN CAMP.

New River Gorge National Park & Preserve

New River Gorge National Park & Preserve is America's newest national park, established in December 2020. Don't let the name fool you; the New River is actually one of the oldest rivers in the world! The New River Gorge Bridge is 876 feet above the New River and was the longest single-span arch bridge in the world for 26 years. Brave visitors can even walk the catwalk underneath the bridge (attached to a harness, of course)!

COLOR THE WEST VIRGINIA STATE QUARTER.

CAN YOU COMPLETE THIS NEW RIVER GORGE NATIONAL PARK & PRESERVE CROSSWORD PUZZLE?

DOWN

1. The state where New River Gorge National Park & Preserve is located

3. The New River _____ Bridge is 876 feet above the New River

ACROSS

2. The park was established in this month in 2020

4. The New River Gorge Bridge is featured on the state _____

5. One of the oldest rivers in the world

6. Visitors can walk the _____ across the bridge

Southeast Region

The Southeast Region includes Alabama, Florida, Georgia, Kentucky, Louisiana, Mississippi, North Carolina, South Carolina, and Tennessee. It has impressive underwater wonders, including shipwrecks, coral reefs, and marine life. On land you will find beaches, swamps, twisting rivers, large caves, and the Appalachian and Blue Ridge Mountains. The Southeast Region's climate is temperate with hot, humid summers and mild winters, and it is known for tropical storms and hurricanes. According to the National Weather Service, no snow has fallen in Key West, Florida, or the US Virgin Islands since weather recording began in 1872! From the bayous of Louisiana to the mountains of North Carolina and the beaches of Florida, the Southeast Region has a great variety of landscapes to explore.

Biscayne National Park

Biscayne National Park is 95 percent underwater, making it perfect for boating, canoeing, and kayaking. This national treasure protects the last living coral reef in the continental United States, which is also the third-largest barrier reef in the world! There are several shipwrecks on the Maritime Heritage Trail that visitors can snorkel or scuba dive to see. Over 600 native fish species live within the park, as well as dolphins, manatees, and whales.

FIND AND CIRCLE THE WORDS BELOW IN THIS BISCAYNE NATIONAL PARK WORD SEARCH.

UNDERWATER

CANOEING

BOATING

SHIPWRECK

DOLPHIN

FISH

BISCAYNE

SNORKEL

MANATEE

REEF

```
P S L W J R F G M B C N Y M D
O N P K D U N K G N F R G A L
G O Q R X Q B R E E F P P L B
N R T L W X I D C F D J M I Y
J K Z U W A O A A O V S S U W
K E E T A N A M L F P C M K V
C L D E N K K P Y V A Y L E Q
E Y E U J J H I X Y E O T W K
R A M G N I E O N A C P T M T
W A H Q N R F E M J H L O S W
P I U O A P V Q E B Y Z H M V
I S L B K U L N Y S O G S C S
H S G T W V A B Y G G T I T C
S C U N D E R W A T E R F S N
B O A T I N G X L D C L F F J
```

CAN YOU FIND THE MANATEE, DOLPHIN, WHALE, TREASURE CHEST, SHARK, SPEARFISH, STURGEON, AND TARPON EEL IN THE SHIPWRECK?

Dry Tortugas National Park

Dry Tortugas National Park protects Fort Jefferson and the seven Dry Tortugas Islands and is accessible only by boat or seaplane. Tortugas is Spanish for "turtles," and dry is from the absence of fresh water. Five types of turtles live at Dry Tortugas: green, loggerhead, Kemp's Ridley, leatherback, and hawksbill. Fort Jefferson is a six-sided fortress made from 16 million bricks. It is the largest brick masonry building in the Western Hemisphere!

TRACE THE NAMES OF THE FIVE TYPES OF TURTLES FOUND AT DRY TORTUGAS NATIONAL PARK.

GREEN

LOGGERHEAD

KEMP'S RIDLEY

LEATHERBACK

HAWKSBILL

START

FINISH

Everglades National Park

Everglades National Park is the largest subtropical wilderness in America. While it may look like a big swamp, it's actually a very slow-moving river that averages only about four to five feet deep. There are nine distinct eco-systems within the park. Many endangered and threatened species call the Everglades home, including the Florida panther. This national park is the only place in the world where both alligators and crocodiles live together! The water of the Everglades provides drinking water for millions of people in Florida.

COLOR THE ANIMALS OF THE EVERGLADES.

TRUE OR FALSE? TEST YOUR KNOWLEDGE ABOUT ALLIGATORS AND CROCODILES! CIRCLE THE RIGHT ANSWER.

1. Alligators and crocodiles do not lay eggs.
TRUE FALSE

2. An alligator grows about 3,000 teeth in a lifetime. TRUE FALSE

3. Large crocodiles can survive for more than a year without eating. TRUE FALSE

4. Crocodiles and alligators can't jump.
TRUE FALSE

5. Alligators and crocodiles have four-chambered hearts like humans. TRUE FALSE

6. Saltwater crocodiles are the smallest reptiles in the world. TRUE FALSE

7. Alligators and crocodiles eat fruit.
TRUE FALSE

8. Alligators prefer fresh water over salt water.
TRUE FALSE

Mammoth Cave National Park

Mammoth Cave is the longest known cave system in the world, with more than 400 miles of cave passageways. Stephen Bishop, an enslaved person, was one of the first to extensively explore and map it. He is credited with important discoveries within the cave, including rivers, many animals, and the Bottomless Pit—a 105-foot-deep cavern. Visitors can marvel at Frozen Niagara, a dripstone formation that looks like a frozen waterfall, and view cave art (called petroglyphs and pictographs) made by early Native Americans.

CAN YOU CRACK THE CODE?

A total of 13 species of bats live within or around Mammoth Cave. Can you crack the code to discover which species is listed below?

＿ ＿ ＿ ＿ ＿ ＿ ＿ ＿ ＿ ＿ ＿ ,
15 6 8 4 5 23 21 18 7 23 21

＿ ＿ ＿ - ＿ ＿ ＿ ＿ ＿ ＿ ＿ ＿
3 4 26 23 6 15 23 17 3 6 2

KEY

1	2	3	4	5	6	7	8	9	10	11	12	13
Z	T	B	I	N	A	U	F	L	C	O	M	H

14	15	16	17	18	19	20	21	22	23	24	25	26
P	R	X	D	Q	V	J	S	W	E	K	Y	G

32

FIND AND CIRCLE THE WORDS BELOW IN THIS MAMMOTH CAVE WORD SEARCH.

```
I N Q J G E F G F N Z C R F K
O M E Y H E F X R U M E Y B E
M P V E P U W P O T L C T U N
H I A S Y B V A Z B W T U M T
W C C Z L I K S E F R U C W U
L T E P G M L S N W M O L Y C
K O F H O R E A N C S K D U K
H G Q F R D J G I B E O H T Y
T R A J T T X E A U W F N R O
O A L T E T R W G F Q H L S C
M P A V P W U A A O S Y Q L O
M H S A M V E Y R B B Y M Q K
A Y R D W P T C A A L H J H J
M Q F F F O R M A T I O N M U
U P O H S I B N E H P E T S G
```

MAMMOTH

CAVE

STEPHEN BISHOP

KENTUCKY

PETROGLYPH

PICTOGRAPH

FROZEN NIAGARA

BAT

PASSAGEWAY

FORMATION

Congaree National Park

Congaree National Park preserves the largest part of an unusual forest (called old-growth bottomland hardwood forest) in the United States. Its champion trees are some of the tallest in the eastern United States and provide one of the highest forest canopies in the world. Visitors can kayak, canoe, or walk on boardwalk trails to see the many beautiful trees, including the loblolly pine, laurel oak, swamp tupelo, and water hickory. In the summer, fireflies put on an incredible show in the evening by lighting up at the same time!

CAN YOU UNSCRAMBLE THESE CONGAREE NATIONAL PARK WORDS?

REEACGNO _____

HSTOU LAAONRCI _____

EORSFT _____

WKAADLORB _____

IRLEYFF _____

LALURE KAO _____

FIND SIX MATCHING PAIRS OF FIREFLIES.

⭐ Great Smoky Mountains National Park

With more than 10 million visitors each year, Great Smoky Mountains National Park is the most visited national park in the United States. It boasts over 800 miles of hiking trails and almost 3,000 miles of streams filled with large trout. The smoky look comes from the millions of plants and trees that give off volatile organic compounds. One of the most popular locations in the park is Cades Cove, with stunning views, wildlife, and historic cabins, churches, and barns. The black bear is the symbol of the Smokies; there are about 1,500 bears in the park.

CIRCLE THE ITEMS YOU WOULD BRING OR WEAR ON A SUMMER HIKE IN GREAT SMOKY MOUNTAINS NATIONAL PARK.

FILL IN THE BLANKS WITH A WORD FROM THE WORD BANK.

1. Great Smoky Mountains National Park is the _____ visited national park.

2. There are over _____ miles of hiking trails.

3. The black _____ is the symbol of the Smokies.

4. _____ is one of the most popular locations in the park.

5. Great Smoky Mountains National Park has over 10 _____ visitors each year.

6. Great Smoky Mountains National Park is located in Tennessee and _____ _____ .

bear	800	most
North Carolina	million	Cades Cove

Virgin Islands National Park

Virgin Islands National Park is located on the island of St. John in the US Virgin Islands, which has coasts on both the Caribbean Sea and the Atlantic Ocean. It is the only place in the US where you drive on the left side of the road. There are rock carvings by the Taino people, who inhabited the island over 1,000 years ago, Danish sugar plantations, 144 species of birds, over 300 species of fish, 748 species of plants, and approximately 40 species of coral within the park.

OVER 1,000 YEARS AGO, THE TAINO PEOPLE ESTABLISHED VILLAGES ON WHAT IS NOW THE US VIRGIN ISLANDS. TRACE THE WORDS BELOW IN THE TAINO LANGUAGE.

FLOWER	ANA
TRUMPET	FOTUTO
BUTTERFLY	TANAMA
FATHER	BABA
WIND	HURSA
MOTHER	BIBI
HUMMINGBIRD	COLIBRI

CONNECT THE DOTS TO DISCOVER THE BEAUTIFUL CORAL!

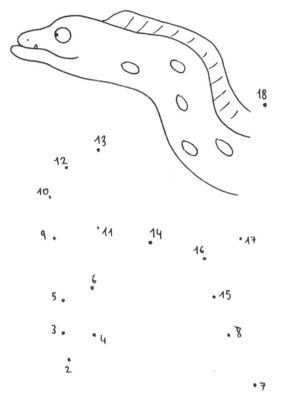

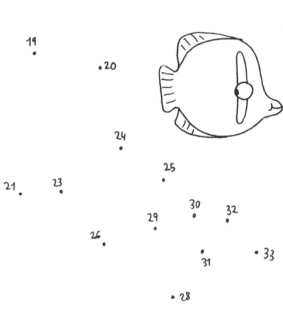

19
•20
18
•24
13
12
25
10
21 23
9 •11 14 29 30 32
16 •17 26 •33
6 31
5 •15 •28
3 •4
8
2
•7 22 27

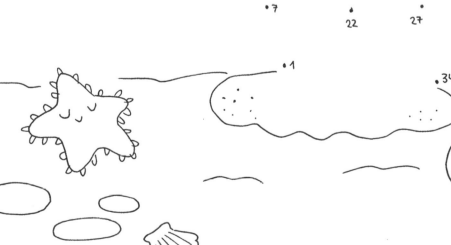

•1
•34

Intermountain Region

The Intermountain Region includes Arizona, Colorado, Montana, New Mexico, Oklahoma, Texas, Utah, and Wyoming. In this area of the United States, you'll find deep canyons, mesas, and colors of red, yellow, brown, and orange from the different soils of the earth. Vast wilderness, painted deserts, dunes, lakes, and mountains are part of this region. The Intermountain Region is home to the first national park and the first national monument! Across the parks in the Intermountain Region, you can see how the environment and humans have played a role in shaping the various landscapes. For example, the Colorado River was instrumental in carving out what we know today as the Grand Canyon. Ancient dwellings, rock art, and petroglyphs in this region also help connect us to our ancestors.

☆ Grand Canyon National Park

The Grand Canyon is a mile deep, 277 miles long, and 18 miles wide. In fact, the Grand Canyon is bigger than the state of Rhode Island! Scientists believe it took about six million years of erosion from the Colorado River and other geologic activity to carve out what we know as the Grand Canyon today. There are about 1,000 caves in this park, but only 335 have been recorded and only one cave has been open to the public. Supai Village, located at the base of the Grand Canyon, is the only place in the United States where mules deliver the mail.

PUT THE FOLLOWING NATIVE AMERICAN TRIBES WITH CONNECTIONS TO THE GRAND CANYON IN ALPHABETICAL ORDER, FROM 1 TO 11.

____ Paiute Indian Tribe of Utah

____ Havasupai Tribe

____ Hualapai Tribe

____ Kaibab Band of Paiute Indians

____ Yavapai-Apache Nation

____ Hopi Tribe

____ Moapa Band of Paiute Indians

____ Navajo Nation

____ San Juan Southern Paiute Tribe

____ Las Vegas Band of Paiute Indians

____ Pueblo of Zuni

CIRCLE THE SIX DIFFERENCES BETWEEN THESE TWO PICTURES OF THE GRAND CANYON.

Petrified Forest National Park

Petrified Forest National Park contains one of the world's largest and most beautiful concentrations of petrified wood in the world. The fallen trees and many fossils found here are from the Late Triassic period, which occurred over 200 million years ago! Petrified wood is a fossil made up almost entirely of quartz from the minerals it absorbed over time. Its stunning colors also come from manganese, iron, and carbon found in the soil. Petrified Forest National Park is the only park that includes part of historic Route 66.

FIND AND CIRCLE THE WORDS BELOW IN THIS PETRIFIED FOREST NATIONAL PARK WORD SEARCH.

PETRIFIED

MANGANESE

QUARTZ

IRON

NATIONAL

PARK

TRIASSIC

WOOD

FOSSIL

ARIZONA

```
J  G  I  V  X  T  W  M  K  H  V  B  V  Y  P
V  G  C  I  S  S  A  I  R  T  W  V  D  A  Z
Z  S  R  M  T  N  E  A  Z  G  D  L  K  T  G
J  O  M  Q  P  N  R  Z  I  A  I  P  B  J  C
N  N  Z  K  U  I  I  J  I  S  Y  E  V  E  Z
V  E  I  Q  Z  A  U  R  S  A  D  T  Q  L  P
W  E  S  O  U  T  R  O  E  S  Q  R  O  J  N
N  L  N  E  Q  F  T  T  K  L  I  U  G  C
Q  A  A  Y  N  G  D  M  Z  B  H  F  U  U  B
N  C  U  N  G  A  V  D  A  V  V  I  W  A  J
J  O  V  C  O  C  G  D  O  S  E  E  S  V  B
T  Z  D  P  Q  I  E  N  P  O  P  D  C  P  V
L  F  A  H  O  T  T  A  A  F  W  D  N  O  E
L  R  M  Z  K  P  B  A  W  M  S  K  Y  Z  K
K  T  L  U  N  Q  G  D  N  N  C  D  Z  Z  N
```

USE YOUR IMAGINATION TO COLOR
THIS PICTURE OF PETRIFIED FOREST
NATIONAL PARK.

Saguaro National Park

Saguaro National Park is divided into two districts: the Rincon Mountain District and the Tucson Mountain District. While the park has 25 types of cacti, it's most famous for the saguaro cactus, which can grow over 40 feet tall and live more than 150 years! Saguaro is home to many animal species, including roadrunners, Gila monsters, kangaroo rats, diamondback rattlesnakes, and horned lizards. The sunsets are particularly stunning.

FILL IN THE MISSING LETTERS.

1. Sa _ ua _ o Nat _ on _ l _ ar _

2. T _ cso _ _ ou _ tai _ Dis _ ri _ t

3. Roa _ ru _ _ e _

4. _ i _ a _ on _ te _

5. K _ ng _ r _ o _ _ t

6. _ ia _ on _ ba _ k r _ tt _ es _ a _ e

7. C _ ct _ s

8. _ ri _ o _ a

USE THE KEY BELOW TO COLOR THE SAGUARO CACTUS.

1	BROWN	3	RED	5	BLUE
2	GREEN	4	YELLOW	6	LIME GREEN

Black Canyon of the Gunnison National Park

Black Canyon of the Gunnison is known for its narrow canyons and tall cliffs. The cliffs are so tall that sunlight doesn't always reach the bottom of the canyons; the park got its name from these dark spaces. The park is also known for Painted Wall, the tallest cliff in Colorado (named for its light-colored bands of rock). It's one of the best places to view the night sky; astronomy ranger programs help aspiring astronomers see the stars. Visitors can learn how to snowshoe with a park ranger in the winter.

CAN YOU UNSCRAMBLE THESE BLACK CANYON OF THE GUNNISON NATIONAL PARK WORDS?

LOROODCA _____

ABLCK NCOANY _____

APIDTEN LALW _____

TNAOYSOMR _____

FLFCSI _____

OEONHSSW _____

Great Sand Dunes National Park & Preserve

Great Sand Dunes National Park & Preserve protects the tallest sand dunes in North America, including Star Dune, which is 741 feet tall from base to crest. Boards and sleds made specifically for dry sand can be rented at the park—surf's up! The sand temperature can be extreme, reaching 150 degrees Fahrenheit in the summer and −20 degrees Fahrenheit in the winter. Did you know you can hear the Earth "sing" at this park? When air creates an avalanche in the sand dunes, millions of tumbling sand grains sound like humming.

MATCH THE CLUES ON THE LEFT SIDE WITH THE CORRECT ANSWERS ON THE RIGHT SIDE.

1. Park location

2. Height of Star Dune

3. Summer temperature of sand

4. You can use this to "surf" the dunes

5. The sound of sand grains moving

A. 741 feet

B. Humming

C. Sand boards

D. 150 degrees Fahrenheit

E. Colorado

COLOR THE GREAT SAND DUNES
JUNIOR RANGER PATCH.

Mesa Verde National Park

Mesa Verde National Park is the largest archaeological preserve in the United States. Due to the surrounding juniper and piñon forest, the area was named Mesa Verde, which is Spanish for "green table." For 700 years, ancient Pueblo built communities into the cliffs (called "cliff dwellings") that you can now visit. Cliff Palace is the largest and best-known cliff dwelling; archaeologists believe that about 100 people lived there. Point Lookout Trail offers incredible views of the La Plata and San Juan Mountains, along with Montezuma and Mancos Valleys.

CONNECT THE DOTS TO SEE WHAT THE CLIFF PALACE LOOKS LIKE.

Cliff Palace is the largest cliff dwelling, but there are four other dwellings you can see at Mesa Verde National Park. Can you use the code to find out what they're called?

3 9 4 12 6 17 26   10 6 11 18 2

4 6 17 19   10 6 11 18 2

18 1 22 11 12 2   24 22 2 2

10 6 11 18 2

18 24 2 1   10 6 11 18 2

KEY

1	2	3	4	5	6	7	8	9	10	11	12	13
P	E	B	L	Q	O	V	F	A	H	U	C	I

14	15	16	17	18	19	20	21	22	23	24	25	26
W	D	K	N	S	G	M	J	R	Z	T	X	Y

☆Rocky Mountain National Park

Visitors will feel like they're on top of the world at Rocky Mountain National Park! Ninety-eight mountains rise above 11,000 feet; Longs Peak is the highest peak in the park at 14,259 feet. Forty-two miles of the Continental Divide—mountains that define the direction rivers flow into oceans and seas—run through the middle of the park. Trail Ridge Road is the highest continuously paved highway in the United States. The park is home to more than 60 mammals, including bighorn sheep, moose, and elk.

CAN YOU MATCH THE ANIMAL TO ITS PAW- OR HOOFPRINT?

1. ___

2. ___

3. ___

4. ___

5. ___

6. ___

A

B

C

D

E

F

CAN YOU COMPLETE THIS ROCKY MOUNTAIN NATIONAL PARK CROSSWORD PUZZLE?

DOWN

2. Ninety-eight _____ rise above 11,000 feet

3. The state in which Rocky Mountain National Park is located

ACROSS

1. The park is home to more than 60 _____

4. Highest peak in Rocky Mountain National Park

5. The highest continuously paved highway in the United States

6. The _____ Divide runs through the middle of the park

Glacier National Park

Glacier National Park protects over one million acres of land carved out by, you guessed it, glaciers. In 1910, the newly established park had around 80 glaciers; today, 26 glaciers remain. Currently, the largest is Harrison Glacier. Lake McDonald, ten miles long and almost 500 feet deep, is the largest lake in the park and is known for its red, green, and blue rocks. From the summit of Triple Divide Peak, water may flow to the Pacific Ocean, Atlantic Ocean, or Hudson Bay. Glacier National Park is part of the world's first international peace park.

FIND AND CIRCLE THE WORDS BELOW IN THIS GLACIER NATIONAL PARK WORD SEARCH.

GLACIER

LAKE McDONALD

PACIFIC

ATLANTIC

HUDSON BAY

MONTANA

PARK

SUMMIT

```
O T K X E J C S Q D Y C W W V
U D Q D X N T Y H L A Q P N Z
B X O C Z P O P W A B F A G R
M M O G J O O B Z N N Y R E G
V W N V S K F Y R O O J K N L
Q H X A M K K N R D S J B R A
P S A T M C C T I C D D V X C
C Z Y L O I A E Q M U J K Y I
S B W A N F L T X E H Y S R E
N T R N T I B K B K H Z K C R
M I E T A C L F S A U R I P T
E M Y I N A F N J L Q K N G A
D M U C A P C Z L I J P F B U
A U W C H M S F F G W X J B E
P S N P L O T I L B H I V T F
```

THE MULTICOLORED ROCKS OF LAKE McDONALD ARE BEAUTIFUL! HAVE FUN COLORING THE PICTURE BELOW.

Carlsbad Caverns National Park

Carlsbad Caverns are located beneath the Chihuahuan Desert. There are more than 119 caves within the park; Lechuguilla Cave is one of the longest caves in the world. Before 1925, visitors were lowered into the caves in a big bucket—thank goodness for elevators! Seventeen species of bats live within the park. During the summer, thousands of bats fly out of the caves all at once each night in search of food.

FILL IN THE BLANKS WITH A WORD FROM THE WORD BANK.

1. The Chihuahuan _____ is found above Carlsbad Caverns.

2. Before 1925, many guests were lowered into the caves by a _____.

3. One of the longest caves in the world is _____.

4. _____ species of bats live in this park.

5. Bats fly out of the caves to search for _____.

6. There are more than _____ caves within the park.

119	Lechuguilla Cave	Desert
food	bucket	17

HOW MANY BATS CAN YOU FIND IN
ONE OF THE CARLSBAD CAVERNS?

White Sands National Park

The sand of White Sands National Park is almost pure gypsum, creating the world's largest gypsum dune field. Unlike typical sand, gypsum doesn't get very hot, even during the summer months. Scientists have found fossil footprints in the park from ancient animals like the Columbian mammoth, dire wolf, and the Harlan's ground sloth. Because the park is next to White Sands Missile Range, it occasionally closes during missile tests.

CAN YOU FIND THE SIX PAIRS OF MATCHING DIRE WOLVES?

CAN YOU UNSCRAMBLE THESE WHITE SANDS NATIONAL PARK WORDS?

MSPGYU ______________________

WTHEI ASDNS ______________________

____

LFOSIS ______________________

FROONTPTI ______________________

MLOBCANUI MOMHTMA ______________________

____

DEIR LWFO ______________________

EWN MEXOIC ______________________

____

Big Bend National Park

Big Bend National Park is named for the "big bend" in the Rio Grande, which runs through the park. Scientists have made some impressive fossil finds at the park, including the bones of a giant pterosaur, the largest known flying creature of all time. A graduate student discovered the bones of the Alamosaurus, a dinosaur that measured 100 feet tall and probably weighed more than 50 tons. The park covers three habitats: river, desert, and mountain. And it's the only park in the US that contains an entire mountain range (the Chisos Mountains)!

TRACE THE NAMES OF SOME OF THE ANIMAL FOSSILS THAT HAVE BEEN DISCOVERED IN BIG BEND NATIONAL PARK.

ALAMOSAURUS

AGUJACERATOPS

BRAVOCERATOPS

QUETZALCOATLUS

DEINOSUCHUS

CONNECT THE DOTS TO SEE WHAT THE ALAMOSAURUS LOOKED LIKE.

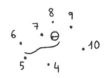

8   9
7
6   ·θ
5   ·4   ·10

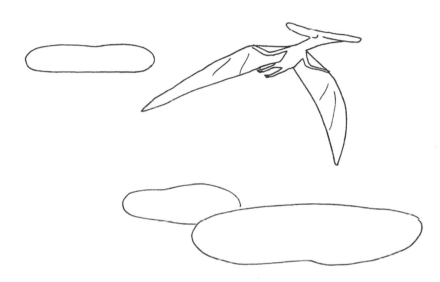

·11

12

·3

·13

17

·2   23   22

·14

18

·16

21

15

1   25   24   20   19

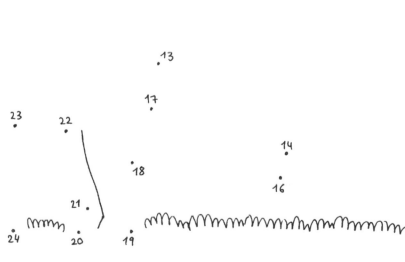

Guadalupe Mountains National Park

Created in 1972, Guadalupe Mountains National Park protects the world's most extensive fossil reef. Millions of years ago, the area around the park was part of an inland sea. The reef was exposed when the sea evaporated, and it now towers above the desert. The park is also known for its bright white Salt Basin Dunes, made of gypsum, which range from 3 to 60 feet high. Guadalupe Peak, known as the "Top of Texas," is the highest point in the entire state!

FILL IN THE MISSING LETTERS.

1. S _ _ t _ asi _ D _ n _ s
2. _ ua _ a _ u _ e
3. _ o _ _ f _ e _ a _
4. G _ _ dal _ _ e _ ea _
5. _ o _ _ il R _ _ f

MATCH THE CLUES ON THE LEFT SIDE WITH THE CORRECT ANSWERS ON THE RIGHT SIDE.

1. Guadalupe Mountains National Park is located in this state

2. Guadalupe Mountains National Park protects this

3. Nickname for Guadalupe Peak

4. What Salt Basin Dunes are made of

5. Year the park was created

A. Fossil reef

B. Top of Texas

C. Texas

D. Gypsum

E. 1972

Arches National Park

Arches National Park is named after and best known for its stone arches. In fact, Arches National Park has the densest concentration of natural stone arches in the world! Landscape Arch has the longest span of any arch in North America. Balanced Rock is a massive sandstone boulder that delicately sits on a pedestal and is estimated to weigh 3,577 tons—that's the weight of approximately 27 blue whales! Like Guadalupe Mountains National Park, the entire area was part of a large inland sea millions of years ago.

YOU CAN MAKE OVER 6,000 WORDS FROM THE LETTERS IN ARCHES NATIONAL PARK. LIST EIGHT NEW WORDS HERE.

1. _____

2. _____

3. _____

4. _____

5. _____

6. _____

7. _____

8. _____

MATCH THE PIECES ON THE LEFT TO THE CORRECT PIECE ON THE RIGHT.

1. ____

2. ____

3. ____

4. ____

A

B

C

D

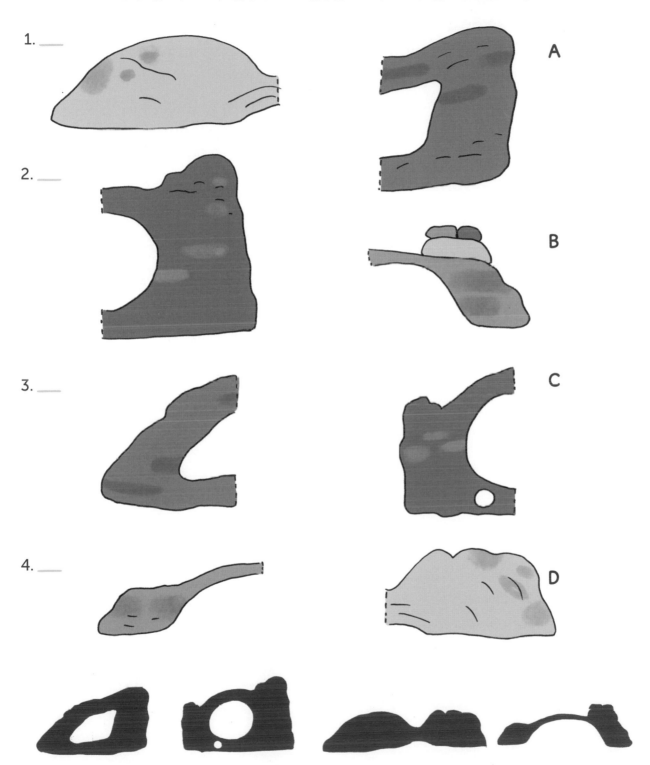

Bryce Canyon National Park

Bryce Canyon National Park has the largest concentration of hoodoos in the world! A hoodoo is a tall, skinny rock formation that gives the park an alien feel. The best-known hoodoo is Thor's Hammer, named for the Norse god of thunder. Due to the park's elevation, there are three different climate zones: ponderosa pine forest, spruce/fir forest, and pinyon/juniper forest. Hopi, Zuni, Navajo, Southern Paiute, and Ute Native Americans have a long history in Bryce Canyon. An asteroid was named after the park in 2007.

FIND AND CIRCLE THE WORDS BELOW IN THIS BRYCE CANYON NATIONAL PARK WORD SEARCH.

BRYCE CANYON

HOODOO

THOR

PONDEROSA

ASTEROID

HOPI

ZUNI

NAVAJO

SOUTHERN PAIUTE

UTE

```
F H O O D O O U T A E O L H F
W H D Z C P V T B F T V O E P
D Z O V U O E E R V U L R A R
I E B P H N S A Y N I U O E X
O Q J C I D I B C D A C H E X
R J B G K E W G E E P V T D T
E F K V S R H U C B N G A I I
T Z Z C R O P Z A H R B H J X
S I S B Z S L A N B E N S K O
A K L A F A R H Y V H N L D R
Q L L L R Y Y A O H T U J N D
G T L H S R U G N S U P R L H
I R G N L M T C Y L O F O D F
Z G W J N P Z W T B S M H N G
J S N S R Q D M X Q G Q H L J
```

CIRCLE THE SIX DIFFERENCES BETWEEN THESE TWO PICTURES OF BRYCE CANYON NATIONAL PARK.

Canyonlands National Park

Canyonlands is Utah's largest national park. The park is divided into land districts, including the Island in the Sky district, which sits on a large mesa offering incredible views of the park. The Needles area is named for the massive red-and-white-banded sandstone pillars that tower over the area. The Maze area of the park is the most remote. The Colorado and Green Rivers run through Canyonlands. Horseshoe Canyon has some of the best-preserved rock art in North America.

TRUE OR FALSE? CIRCLE THE RIGHT ANSWER.

1. Canyonlands is Utah's smallest national park.
TRUE FALSE

2. The Island in the Sky district sits on a large mesa. TRUE FALSE

3. The Maze district is the most remote area of the park. TRUE FALSE

4. The Red River runs through Canyonlands National Park. TRUE FALSE

5. Horseshoe Canyon has some of the best-preserved rock art in North America. TRUE FALSE

CAN YOU COMPLETE THIS CANYONLANDS NATIONAL PARK CROSSWORD PUZZLE?

DOWN

1. District with well-preserved rock art

2. Most remote district

4. Canyonlands National Park is located in this state

ACROSS

3. District with massive sandstone pillars

5. One of two rivers that runs through Canyonlands

6. District that sits on a large mesa

Capitol Reef National Park

Early settlers thought the white sandstone domes in the area looked like the dome of the Capitol building in Washington, DC, and the cliffs and canyons were like a "barrier reef"—difficult to cross. And just like that, the name Capitol Reef was born. Waterpocket Fold, a distinctive feature of the park, is a wrinkle in the earth's crust (called a geologic monocline) that consists of mountains, canyons, arches, and natural bridges. It runs for almost 100 miles!

FILL IN THE MISSING LETTERS.

1. _ et _ le _ s
2. N _ t _ r _ l _ r _ d _ e
3. Wr _ _ kl _
4. _ at _ r _ o _ k _ t _ _o _ d
5. Mo _ o _ li _ e
6. _ t _ h
7. _ a _ it _ l _ ee _

USE YOUR IMAGINATION TO COLOR IN THIS
PICTURE OF CAPITOL REEF NATIONAL PARK.

⭐Zion National Park

Zion became Utah's first national park in 1919. One of the park's most popular areas is the Narrows, named because it's the narrowest section of Zion Canyon. The canyon, which is 2,000 feet deep, features red-and-cream-colored walls made of sandstone, eroded by the Virgin River. The sandstone cliffs lure hikers and rock climbers from all over the world. Angels Landing is one of the most dramatic hikes in the United States, with an incredible view at the top.

CAN YOU CRACK THE CODE?

Before it became a national park, Zion was called something else. Can you use the code to discover what Zion's first name was?

8	26	5	26	16	22	26	11	14	2	25

16	2	22	24	13	16	2	20

8	13	16	26	8	14	16	22

KEY

1	2	3	4	5	6	7	8	9	10	11	12	13
C	A	Y	R	K	D	Z	M	B	F	W	H	O

14	15	16	17	18	19	20	21	22	23	24	25	26
E	J	N	S	V	G	L	Q	T	X	I	P	U

FIND YOUR WAY THROUGH THE MAZE TO THE TOP OF ANGELS LANDING!

FINISH

START

★ Grand Teton National Park

Grand Teton National Park protects the major peaks within the Teton Range, the youngest mountain range within the Rocky Mountains. Like in other mountainous areas across the United States, glaciers helped carve out many peaks and valleys in the park, including Grand Teton, which stands at 13,775 feet above sea level. The park is also a large nature conservatory filled with elk, bison, coyotes, wolves, eagles, foxes, and bears. Grand Teton is the only national park with a commercial airport located within its grounds!

USE YOUR IMAGINATION TO COLOR
THE PARK'S ANIMALS.

CAN YOU UNSCRAMBLE THESE GRAND TETON NATIONAL PARK WORDS?

IYONWGM _____

ROIARTP _____

ALRICEG _____

ARGDN TOETN _____

_____

OTCEOY _____

INSBO _____

EGLEA _____

☆Yellowstone National Park

Yellowstone became the first national park on March 1, 1872. Covering 2.2 million acres, it's home to more geysers than anywhere else in the world (Old Faithful is the most famous), multicolored hot springs, petrified trees, and more wildlife than any other park in the lower 48 states. It's located in Idaho, Montana, and Wyoming, and sits above a huge dormant supervolcano that provides the heated water that forms the geysers, hot springs, steam vents, and mud pots.

FIND AND CIRCLE THE WORDS BELOW IN THIS YELLOWSTONE WORD SEARCH.

GEYSER

OLD FAITHFUL

MUD POT

STEAM VENTS

VOLCANO

HOT SPRING

PETRIFIED

WYOMING

```
W W B O G D E I F I R T E P V
Q G U M N V F V T F F Q Y O U
X D M H I H U Q H H W O C X S
I C G M R I K C J D Q D M T Y
P Z N U P M D Y T V Z W N L X
L I I D S N S L S T P E U X V
U T M P T D P R K O V F T L O
G V O O O Z J S Z M H H G B L
S D Y T H V N O A T N A W P C
O A W D B O K E I R E U P R A
L Y H Y D G T A C Q P I E E N
I T H Z Q S F K L O Y Y E S O
V U Y X W D A D E H C M M Y F
B T K P L Z P K Z K N M W E G
H K Q O P P F Y S Z Q H Z G P
```

78

COLOR GRAND PRISMATIC SPRING, NAMED FOR THE RAINBOW COLORS CAUSED BY MICROSCOPIC ORGANISMS, USING THE KEY BELOW.

1 BROWN   3 YELLOW   5 BLUE
2 ORANGE   4 GREEN

Pacific Region

The Pacific Region includes American Samoa, California, Hawaii, Idaho, Nevada, Oregon, and Washington. As part of an area known as the Ring of Fire, this region features forces of nature like volcanoes and earthquakes. On the other end of the temperature spectrum, several parts of this region were shaped by glaciers. Some locations receive a lot of snow, while others are much more temperate. Enormous trees, deep lakes, rainforests, islands formed from lava, and even some deserts cover this area. The Pacific Region is home to many amazing animals, like the island fox and scrub jay, that are found nowhere else on Earth, as well as several different cultures and languages.

National Park of American Samoa

National Park of American Samoa is the only national park south of the equator. It spans three islands in the South Pacific: Tutuila, Ta'ū, and Ofu. The park protects tropical rainforests, coral reefs, and the flying fox, but surprise—the flying fox is actually a bat! Three species of bats are the only native mammals in this archipelago, including large fruit bats with three-foot wingspans. In addition to protecting natural resources, this national park also helps to preserve the customs, beliefs, and traditions of the Samoan culture, the oldest in Polynesia.

CIRCLE WHAT YOU WOULD WEAR ON YOUR VISIT TO THIS HOT PARK.

LEARN COMMON WORDS IN THE SAMOAN
LANGUAGE BY TRACING THEM BELOW.
THE PRONUNCIATIONS ARE IN PARENTHESES.

HELLO
TALOFA (TAR-LOW-FAR)

GOODBYE
TOFA (TORE-FAR)

THANK YOU
FA'AFETAI (FAR-AH-FAY-TIE)

YES
IOE (EE-OH-E)

NO
LEAI (LE-AH-E)

GOOD NIGHT
MANUIA LE PO
(MAR-NU-E-AH LE POH)

Channel Islands National Park

Channel Islands National Park consists of five islands in the Pacific Ocean: Anacapa Island, known for Arch Rock and a historic lighthouse; Santa Cruz Island, home to Painted Cave, one of the largest sea caves in the world; Santa Rosa Island, with rare Torrey pines and sandstone canyons; San Miguel Island, which protects one of the world's largest rookeries of sea lions and seals; and Santa Barbara Island, the smallest island, which provides nesting sites for endangered California brown pelicans. The island fox is found only in the Channel Islands, and the island scrub jay is found only on Santa Cruz Island.

THE NATIVE PEOPLE OF CHANNEL ISLANDS, THE CHUMASH, ARE KNOWN FOR THEIR IMPRESSIVE BASKETRY SKILLS. FIND THE MATCHING BASKETS.

CAN YOU COMPLETE THIS CHANNEL ISLANDS CROSSWORD PUZZLE?

DOWN

1. Torrey pines are found on this island

4. This is the smallest island

6. Painted Cave is found on this island

8. The state where the Channel Islands are located

ACROSS

2. This ocean surrounds Channel Islands National Park

3. Sea lions and seals are found on this island

5. A historic lighthouse is found on this island

7. This bird is found only on Santa Cruz Island

Death Valley National Park

Death Valley National Park is the hottest, driest, and lowest national park. The hottest air temperature ever recorded in Death Valley was 134 degrees Fahrenheit on July 10, 1913! And the park's Badwater Basin is the lowest point in North America, at 282 feet below sea level. It is the largest national park in the contiguous United States. Popular stopping points include Artists Palette, which has many colors, including beautiful shades of red, blue, and green, created from volcanic deposits. In addition, the park has many historical relics, like mines, kilns, and ghost towns.

FILL IN THE BLANKS WITH A WORD FROM THE WORD BANK.

1. The lowest point in North America is _____ _____.

2. The multicolored hills are called _____.

3. Death Valley is the _____, driest, and lowest national park.

4. The hottest air temperature recorded in Death Valley was _____.

5. Historical relics include _____.

6. Death Valley National Park is located in _____.

134 degrees	Badwater Basin	ghost towns
hottest	California	Artists Palette

START

HELP THE DESERT
BIGHORN SHEEP
GET DOWN FROM
THE MOUNTAIN IN
DEATH VALLEY.

FINISH

☆ Joshua Tree National Park

Joshua Tree National Park's namesake isn't really a tree. A Joshua tree is a species of yucca. The unusually shaped Joshua tree has an average life span of 150 years and can even grow roots from its branches! From Keys View, visitors can see Coachella Valley, the San Andreas Fault, and on a clear day, Signal Mountain in Mexico. There are 46 species of reptiles found within the park, including desert iguana, yellow-backed spiny lizard, California kingsnake, southwestern speckled rattlesnake, and the endangered Mojave desert tortoise.

JOSHUA TREES CAN BE MANY DIFFERENT SIZES AND SHAPES. CAN YOU FIND THE MATCHING JOSHUA TREES?

1. The Joshua tree is a species of yucca.
    TRUE FALSE

2. The Joshua tree has an average life span of
    300 years. TRUE FALSE

3. From Keys View, visitors can see Coachella
    Valley. TRUE FALSE

4. Joshua Tree National Park is located in Ohio.
    TRUE FALSE

5. There are 46 species of reptiles found within
    the park. TRUE FALSE

6. The New York kingsnake can be found in
    the park. TRUE FALSE

Kings Canyon National Park

Kings Canyon National Park shares a boundary with Sequoia National Park (see page 98) in California's Sierra Nevada. It is home to incredible giant sequoia trees and fascinating wildlife. The park's General Grant is the second largest tree by volume in the world (46,608 cubic feet). There are 72 species of mammals that live in both parks, including mule deer, mountain lions, bats, and black bears. Kings Canyon also has the largest remaining grove of sequoia trees in the world.

COLOR THE ANIMALS FOUND IN KINGS CANYON NATIONAL PARK.

MATCH THE CLUES ON THE LEFT SIDE WITH THE CORRECT ANSWERS ON THE RIGHT SIDE.

1. Kings Canyon shares a boundary with this park

   A. General Grant

2. The second largest tree by volume

   B. 72

3. Kings Canyon has the largest remaining grove of these

   C. Sequoia trees

4. The state in which Kings Canyon is located

   D. Sequoia National Park

5. The number of species of mammals in both Kings Canyon and Sequoia national parks

   E. Sierra Nevada

6. The mountain range in the park

   F. California

Lassen Volcanic National Park

Lassen Volcanic National Park is one of the few places in the world where you can find all four types of volcanoes: shield, plug dome, composite, and cinder cone. In fact, Lassen Peak is one of the world's largest plug dome volcanoes! Steam vents located under Boiling Springs Lake keep the water temperature around 125 degrees Fahrenheit. The Sulphur Works hydro-thermal area has a distinctive smell and incredible colors. Devastated Area Trail tells the story of the 1915–1916 Lassen Peak eruption and its impact on the land.

CAN YOU CRACK THE CODE?

The Maidu people called Lassen Peak "Kohm Yah-mah-nee." Can you use the code to find out what it means?

___ ___ ___ ___
25 16 12 24

___ ___ ___ ___ ___ ___ ___ ___
7   12 21 16 17 10 4   16

KEY

1	2	3	4	5	6	7	8	9	10	11	12	13
X	B	L	I	Y	G	M	E	Q	A	K	O	F

14	15	16	17	18	19	20	21	22	23	24	25	26
C	J	N	T	Z	D	P	U	H	R	W	S	V

LEARN HOW TO DRAW AN ERUPTING VOLCANO!

NOW DRAW ONE ON YOUR OWN!

Pinnacles National Park

Pinnacles National Park was once part of a volcanic field that was roughly 200 miles away from where it is today. Due to tectonic forces, the volcanic field moved along the San Andreas Fault to its current location. Erosion, tectonic movement, and water helped to create the rock formations—the Pinnacles—that make up the park today. The park is also known for its talus caves, which were created when huge boulders fell into deep canyons and created passageways, or newly formed caves. There are almost 500 species of bees within the park, making Pinnacles the highest known bee-diversity-per-unit area of any place on Earth.

YOU CAN MAKE MORE THAN 5,000 WORDS FROM THE LETTERS IN PINNACLES NATIONAL PARK. LIST EIGHT NEW WORDS HERE.

1. _____

2. _____

3. _____

4. _____

5. _____

6. _____

7. _____

8. _____

BZZZZZ! FIND THE MATCHING PAIRS OF BEES.

Redwood National Park

Redwood National Park is a combination of a national park and three state parks: Del Norte Coast, Prairie Creek, and Jedediah Smith. The combined parks, known as Redwood National and State Parks, protect forests of redwood trees, the tallest trees in the world. In fact, within the park is a tree named Hyperion, which is thought to be the tallest living tree in the world at 380 feet tall! However, its location is kept secret to protect it. Several scenic drives feature the colossal old-growth redwoods, Crescent Beach, the Pacific Ocean, meadows filled with wildflowers, and grazing Roosevelt elk.

FILL IN THE MISSING LETTERS.

1. D_l No_te Coa_t
2. Pr_irie Cr_e_
3. Je_e_i_h Sm_t_
4. Hy_erio_
5. _res_ent _each
6. Pa_i_i_ O_ea_
7. R_o_e_e_t E_k

EACH RING ON A FALLEN OR CUT TREE REPRESENTS ONE YEAR. COUNT THE RINGS OF THESE TREE STUMPS. HOW OLD IS EACH TREE?

TREE A _____

TREE B _____

TREE C _____

Sequoia National Park

Sequoia National Park (see Kings Canyon National Park, page 90) was the first park created to protect a living organism—the sequoia tree. Giant sequoia trees are the largest trees in the world, as measured by volume (rather than height). General Sherman is the world's largest tree, at 52,508 cubic feet. It lives in the Giant Forest, which is home to five of the ten largest trees in the world. A large granite dome rock called Moro Rock is in the center of the park. The park's eastern border is Mount Whitney, the tallest mountain in the lower 48 states.

FIND AND CIRCLE THE WORDS BELOW IN THIS SEQUOIA NATIONAL PARK WORD SEARCH.

SEQUOIA

GENERAL
SHERMAN

TREE

MORO ROCK

MT. WHITNEY

CALIFORNIA

GIANT
FOREST

GRANITE

MOUNTAIN

```
N A R M K Z B E D A C Z R N C
C A K B Y E N T I H W T M Q A
U L M Z V W A N C G S K K S N
T B O R O F R J N I U I E G O
G Q W I E O P J N A W U M Q K
L R H F F H E N Y N M I J F C
G G A I I O S X N T E L O F O
N X L N N O L L I F V V X D R
C A B G I X M A A O E C M V O
C S B Q W T I J T R B B G R R
I R L W U O E R N E E Q T P O
N I J J U N G L U S T N B J M
G X C Q C W E A O T I R E I T
Q R E Q P B E O M M J M E G G
V S U F F T V T S D E H C E G
```

CONNECT THE
DOTS TO SEE WHAT
GENERAL SHERMAN
LOOKS LIKE.

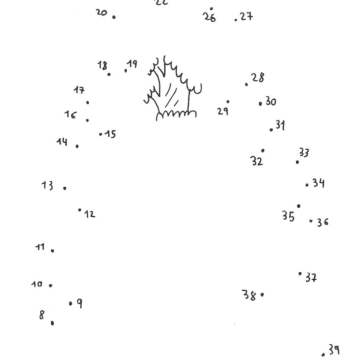

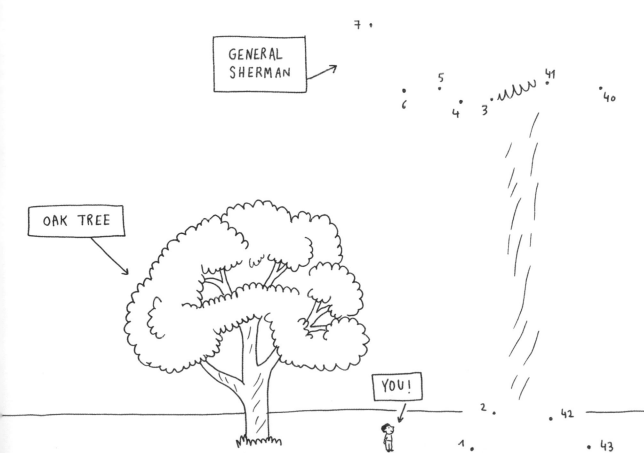

GENERAL
SHERMAN

OAK TREE

YOU!

Yosemite National Park

Yosemite National Park is famous for its granite formations, stunning valleys, sequoia trees, and waterfalls. In fact, Yosemite Falls is one of the tallest waterfalls in the world! Horsetail Fall looks like it's on fire when it glows from the sunset. On a clear full-moon evening, there can be enough light to create a rainbowlike "moonbow" in the waterfall's mist. Mariposa Grove is home to over 500 giant sequoias. The most famous is the Grizzly Giant, standing over 200 feet tall and estimated to be around 3,000 years old.

COLOR THE YOSEMITE JUNIOR RANGER BADGE.

Before the establishment of the National Park Service, the military managed the parks. Can you use the code to see which group was among the first park rangers at Yosemite?

$$\overline{4} \quad \overline{14} \quad \overline{16} \quad \overline{16} \quad \overline{7} \quad \overline{5} \quad \overline{10}$$

$$\overline{26} \quad \overline{10} \quad \overline{5} \quad \overline{15} \quad \overline{17} \quad \overline{11} \quad \overline{23} \quad \overline{26}$$

KEY

1	2	3	4	5	6	7	8	9	10	11	12	13
G	W	J	B	L	N	A	Y	C	O	E	Z	P

14	15	16	17	18	19	20	21	22	23	24	25	26
U	D	F	I	Q	T	H	M	V	R	K	X	S

Haleakalā National Park

Haleakalā National Park, on the island of Maui, is named for the Haleakalā volcano. In Hawaiian, Haleakalā means "house of the sun," and the sunrises and sunsets at the park are stunning. The park has two districts: the Summit District and the coastal Kīpahulu District. Hiking Keonehe'ehe'e (Sliding Sands) Trail in the Summit District gives visitors a view from the crater floor of a volcano. The Kīpahulu District features a bamboo forest and waterfalls, including the beautiful Makahiku Falls. The rare Haleakalā silversword plant, which blooms just once in its lifetime, is found only in Hawaii.

FILL IN THE BLANKS WITH A WORD FROM THE WORD BANK.

1. The park is named for the Haleakalā _____.

2. Haleakalā means "house of the _____."

3. In the Kīpahulu District you can hike through a _____ forest.

4. The Haleakalā _____ only blooms once in its lifetime.

5. The two districts in the park are the Kīpahulu District and the _____ District.

6. The park is located in _____.

Hawaii	silversword	Summit
sun	bamboo	volcano

USE THE KEY BELOW TO COLOR THE HALEAKALĀ SILVERSWORD.

1 SILVER   3 LIME GREEN   5 RED

2 BLUE   4 PINK   6 BROWN

Hawai'i Volcanoes National Park

Hawai'i Volcanoes National Park contains two active volcanoes: Kilauea, the youngest and most active on the island of Hawaii, and Mauna Loa, one of the world's largest shield volcanoes. Mauna Loa rises 30,000 feet from the bottom of the ocean. It's so large that the ocean floor actually bends from its weight! Kealakomo Overlook offers an incredible view of the Pacific Ocean and a vast lava field. Crater Rim Drive leads to craters, a caldera, a steaming bluff, a lava tube, and important sites in Native Hawaiian culture.

CAN YOU UNSCRAMBLE THESE HAWAI'I VOLCANOES NATIONAL PARK WORDS?

AONVSLEOC _____

HIAWIA _____

AKIUALE _____

UANAM OAL _____

ARCERT _____

ICAFICP AEONC _____

CIRCLE THE SIX DIFFERENCES BETWEEN THESE TWO PICTURES OF HAWAI'I VOLCANOES NATIONAL PARK.

Great Basin National Park

This park gets its name from the Great Basin, the mountainous region between the Wasatch Mountains and the Sierra Nevada. It's home to the only glacier in Nevada, Wheeler Peak Glacier, and is best known for the Great Basin bristlecone pine tree, the oldest nonclonal species (which means the trunk is as old as the roots) on Earth. Prometheus, the remains of a Great Basin bristlecone pine, is estimated to be 4,700 to 5,000 years old! At two miles long, Lehman Caves is the longest cave in Nevada. Upper Pictograph Cave shows off pictographs (rock paintings) left behind by the Fremont Indians.

ADD YOUR OWN DRAWINGS TO THE CAVE WALL IN UPPER PICTOGRAPH CAVE.

1. The Great Basin is between the _____ Mountains and the Sierra Nevada.

2. The park is best known for the Great Basin _____ pine.

3. _____ is estimated to be 4,700 to 5,000 years old.

4. Great Basin is home to the only _____ in Nevada.

5. The longest cave in Nevada is _____ _____.

6. Upper Pictograph Cave has ancient rock paintings by the _____ Indians.

Fremont   bristlecone   glacier

Wasatch   Lehman Caves   Prometheus

Crater Lake National Park

About 7,700 years ago, a large volcano erupted and collapsed, forming a big lake now known as Crater Lake, the centerpiece of Crater Lake National Park. Famous for its beautiful blue water, it's the deepest lake in the United States. Wizard Island is a volcanic cone that forms an island in the lake (and looks like a wizard's hat coming out of the water). The Mazama newt lives only on Wizard Island and along the shores of Crater Lake.

FILL IN THE MISSING LETTERS.

1. Vol _ a _ o
2. _ izar _ I _ land
3. V _ lcan _ c co _ e
4. _ a _ e
5. Ma _ am _ ne _ t
6. O _ eg _ n
7. Co _ la _ sed

CRATER LAKE IS FEATURED ON OREGON'S STATE QUARTER. USE YOUR IMAGINATION TO COLOR IT.

Mount Rainier National Park

Mount Rainier is the highest volcanic peak in the contiguous United States. It is an active volcano that has erupted many times over the past half million years. It has the largest glacier system (25 major glaciers) in the lower 48 states; Emmons Glacier has the largest area of any glacier in the park. Yakama, Squaxin Island, Muckleshoot, Nisqually, Cowlitz, Coast Salish, and Puyallup Native Americans all have long associations with this location, and the park reserves special areas for their worship and rituals. In summer, meadows of wildflowers bloom in every color!

YOU CAN MAKE OVER 3,000 WORDS FROM THE LETTERS IN MOUNT RAINIER NATIONAL PARK. LIST EIGHT NEW WORDS HERE.

1. _____

2. _____

3. _____

4. _____

5. _____

6. _____

7. _____

8. _____

USE THE KEY BELOW TO COLOR THE WILDFLOWERS FOUND IN MOUNT RAINIER NATIONAL PARK.

1 GREEN   **3** PURPLE   **5** RED

2 YELLOW   **4** WHITE   **6** BLUE

North Cascades National Park

North Cascades National Park is home to more than 300 glaciers and more than 500 lakes and ponds. The park is one of the snowiest places on Earth and is second only to Alaska in number of glaciers. The park also features the mountain peaks of the North Cascades Range and huge forests. Seventy-five species of mammals live within the park, including the lynx, gray wolf, grizzly bear, river otter, pika, wolverine, and bobcat. A research program in the park studies climate change through the effects of glaciers retreating.

TRUE OR FALSE?
CIRCLE THE RIGHT ANSWER.

1. North Cascades National Park has more than 1,000 glaciers. TRUE FALSE

2. This park has more than 500 lakes and ponds. TRUE FALSE

3. North Cascades National Park is one of the snowiest places on Earth. TRUE FALSE

4. Toucans live within this park. TRUE FALSE

5. Otters live in the park. TRUE FALSE

6. North Cascades National Park is located in Idaho. TRUE FALSE

MATCH THE NAME OF THE ANIMAL WITH THE CORRECT PICTURE AND COLOR THEM IN.

1. _____

2. _____

3. _____

4. _____

5. _____

6. _____

WOLVERINE   GRIZZLY BEAR   LYNX

WOLF   RIVER OTTER   PIKA

☆Olympic National Park

Visitors can experience mountains, beaches, and forests on a trip to Olympic National Park on Washington's Olympic Peninsula. Starfish and anemones live in tide pools and migrating gray whales feed off the coast and can be seen from the beach. Hoh Rain Forest, with tall trees and moss-covered ground, is one of the few remaining temperate rainforests in the United States. Lake Crescent's water is clear 60 feet down in some places! There are over 650 archaeological sites and 130 historic structures in the park.

CAN YOU UNSCRAMBLE THESE OLYMPIC NATIONAL PARK WORDS?

OHH RIAN TEOFSR _____

LKAE TECESRCN _____

TAMIUNNO _____

SECEHBA _____

AITSFSHR _____

YGRA HWEAL _____

OISTNHGNAW _____

THE OLYMPIC MARMOT IS FOUND ONLY ON THE OLYMPIC PENINSULA. HOW MANY OLYMPIC MARMOTS CAN YOU FIND?

Midwest Region

The Midwest Region covers Arkansas, Illinois, Indiana, Iowa, Kansas, Michigan, Minnesota, Missouri, Nebraska, North Dakota, Ohio, South Dakota, and Wisconsin. The parks in this region feature spectacular lakes, hot springs, caves, sand dunes, and even human-made structures. Visitors to the nine parks in this region will find not only some of the oldest sites in the national park system, but also some of the newer sites. Temperatures in the Midwest Region can be a study in extremes, with winter climates among the coldest in the United States. In fact, the only site within the entire national park system that closes in the winter is in this region. Native American history and culture are abundant throughout the Midwest Region.

Hot Springs National Park

The land that became Hot Springs National Park was the first piece of land preserved by the federal government (in 1832). Though it didn't become a national park until 1921, it's the oldest protected area in the national park system. The park features approximately 47 natural hot springs that maintain an average water temperature of 143 degrees Fahrenheit. The water in the hot springs today is from rainwater that fell 4,400 years ago! Hot Springs National Park is the only national park required to give away its primary natural resource to the public.

HAVE FUN COLORING THE HOT SPRINGS JUNIOR RANGER PATCH!

You can soak in the thermal waters at two different bathhouses in the park. Can you use the code to discover their names?

$\overline{12}\ \overline{3}\ \overline{10}\ \overline{21}\ \overline{10}\ \overline{23}$

$\overline{4}\ \overline{3}\ \overline{2}\ \overline{24}\ \overline{13}\ \overline{1}\ \overline{10}\ \overline{6}\ \overline{6}$

KEY

1	2	3	4	5	6	7	8	9	10	11	12	13
T	C	U	B	R	F	L	Z	M	A	I	Q	S

14	15	16	17	18	19	20	21	22	23	24	25	26
D	J	G	O	V	E	X	P	H	W	K	Y	N

Indiana Dunes National Park

Indiana Dunes is made up of swamps, bogs, rivers, dunes, prairies, oak savannas, and marshes. It is filled with 1,960 species of reptiles, fish, mammals, amphibians, and plants, making it one of the most biodiverse areas in the country. With more than 350 species of birds, the park is popular with bird-watchers. It boasts 15 miles of beach along Lake Michigan and acres of sand dunes just inland from the beach. The black oak savannas—grasslands where fire-resistant oak trees live among prairie plants—are some of the last surviving of their kind in the world.

TWEET-TWEET! CAN YOU FIND THE SIX PAIRS OF MATCHING BIRDS?

FIND AND CIRCLE THE WORDS BELOW IN THIS INDIANA DUNES NATIONAL PARK WORD SEARCH.

```
V N A N A I D N I U N T N M X
N K U H Q V C M F A H T N E R
R A H T B J H N M O I D U N E
F U G T F Q D P T X Y F N Q C
K H M I J B H T N K H A C D R
T M S P H I P I I E E N C C I
U O C R B C E U P C N Z W N V
G J M I A B I O D I V E R S E
M O A Q V M R M P G L D Z N R
Y N M P V L I M E X J L U Z X
S U U Q D A F P K H F P A I
N I B U V W R U J E A R U C O
V A E I S G P I A G Y L P A O
Z J S Q R L M K Q C O N C Y T
O S X Y R D Q E T U B B S U O
```

INDIANA	DUNE	LAKE MICHIGAN
SWAMP	PRAIRIE	AMPHIBIANS
BOG	MARSH	BIODIVERSE
RIVER	BIRD	

Isle Royale National Park

Isle Royale National Park covers one large island, part of Lake Superior, and more than 450 smaller islands. It is accessible only by boat or sea-plane. Due to extreme weather, it closes during the winter season—the only national park to do so. Only 19 species of mammals live on the islands. Gray wolves arrived in the 1940s by crossing an ice bridge. Today, the study of wolves on Isle Royale is the longest-running large-mammal predator-prey study in the world. There are four lighthouses within the park, including Rock Harbor Lighthouse, which was completed in 1855.

USE YOUR IMAGINATION TO COLOR THE ISLE ROYALE EMBLEM.

CAN YOU COMPLETE THIS ISLE ROYALE NATIONAL PARK CROSSWORD PUZZLE?

DOWN

1. The state where Isle Royale National Park is located

2. Only 19 species of _____ live on the islands

4. Isle Royale is the only national park that closes during this season

7. There are more than 450 small _____ in the park

ACROSS

3. This animal arrived on Isle Royale in the 1940s

5. Isle Royale is accessible by seaplane or _____

6. Isle Royale is surrounded by Lake _____

Voyageurs National Park

Voyageurs National Park is located in northern Minnesota along the US–Canada border. It is named after the French-Canadian voyageurs (travelers) who used the vast waterways for trade. Almost 40 percent of the park is made up of the Kabetogama, Sand Point, Namakan, and Rainy Lakes, which are filled with 54 different fish species. On a clear night, the aurora borealis can provide a spectacular light show with green, purple, yellow, red, or blue lights dancing in the sky.

CAN YOU FIND THE SIX PAIRS OF MATCHING FISH?

CAN YOU UNSCRAMBLE THESE VOYAGEURS NATIONAL PARK WORDS?

RSVEYAUGO _____

NINMTOSEA _____

ETRSRLAEV _____

DNSA TONIP _____

YRINA ALEK _____

IFSH _____

ITSHGL _____

RRAUAO RLBEISAO _____

Gateway Arch National Park

Gateway Arch National Park, located in downtown St. Louis, is an urban national park. The arch, completed in 1965, was created as a monument to westward expansion in the 19th century. It is the tallest arch in the world and the tallest human-made monument in the United States, and it is as tall as it is wide (630 feet)! At the top of the arch, there are 16 windows on each side of the arch, offering spectacular views of the Mississippi River and St. Louis.

YOU CAN MAKE OVER 5,800 WORDS OUT OF THE LETTERS IN GATEWAY ARCH NATIONAL PARK. LIST EIGHT NEW WORDS HERE.

1. _____

2. _____

3. _____

4. _____

5. _____

6. _____

7. _____

8. _____

HAVE FUN COLORING THE GATEWAY ARCH AND ITS SURROUNDINGS!

Theodore Roosevelt National Park

Theodore Roosevelt National Park features Theodore Roosevelt's first cabin (Maltese Cross) and the remains of his second cabin (Elkhorn Ranch). It is the only national park named for a person. The American bison, once almost extinct, was reintroduced to the park in 1956 and now thrives. Many fossils have been found within the park, including the remains of the Champsosaurus, a 10-foot-long predator similar to a crocodile. Theodore Roosevelt National Park is one of the few national parks where you can see free-roaming horses.

MATCH THE CLUES ON THE LEFT SIDE WITH THE CORRECT ANSWERS ON THE RIGHT SIDE.

1. Roosevelt's second cabin

2. They were nearly extinct, but now thrive

3. A 10-foot-long predator fossil

4. Theodore Roosevelt's first cabin

5. The state where Theodore Roosevelt National Park is located

A. American bison

B. Maltese Cross

C. North Dakota

D. Elkhorn Ranch

E. Champsosaurus

☆Cuyahoga Valley National Park

Cuyahoga Valley National Park preserves the Cuyahoga River's historic, scenic, and natural resources. Most believe that Cuyahoga comes from the Native American Mohawk word Cayagaga, which means "crooked river." The Towpath Trail traces the route of the Ohio and Erie Canals, while Ledges Trail features stunning rock formations leading to Ledges Overlook, which offers fantastic views of the Cuyahoga Valley. One of the park's most popular areas is Brandywine Falls, a 60-foot waterfall that flows into the Brandywine Gorge. The Cuyahoga Valley Scenic Railroad winds through the park.

CAN YOU UNSCRAMBLE THESE CUYAHOGA VALLEY NATIONAL PARK WORDS?

OHOI _____

OACUAYGH YVEALL _____

AIRLORAD _____

IEWBNANRDY LASFL _____

GELESD LOVOKERO _____

DRCOEOK EIRVR _____

COLOR THE CUYAHOGA VALLEY
SCENIC RAILROAD TRAIN.

Badlands National Park

Badlands National Park protects 244,000 acres of mixed-grass prairie, buttes, spires, and pinnacles. Millions of years ago, this area was underwater. As the sea became a subtropical forest and then a savanna, large amounts of sediment were left behind. Water from the Black Hills began to carve dramatic valleys and formations through the sediment, creating the Badlands as we know them today. The Lakota people (Oglala Sioux), who have lived in this area for eons, called this area Mako Sica, or "bad lands."

CAN YOU CRACK THE CODE?

The fastest land mammal in North America is found at Badlands National Park. Can you use the code to discover its name?

25	10	7	17	21	4	7	10	17

KEY

1	2	3	4	5	6	7	8	9	10	11	12	13
M	E	S	H	B	L	O	D	W	R	C	U	T

14	15	16	17	18	19	20	21	22	23	24	25	26
A	F	J	N	Y	K	Q	G	V	Z	I	P	X

THE PRAIRIE RATTLESNAKE LIVES IN BADLANDS
NATIONAL PARK. LEARN HOW TO DRAW ONE
BY FOLLOWING THE STEPS BELOW.

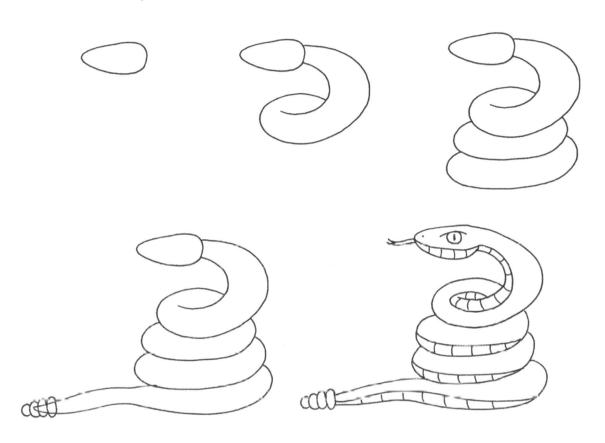

NOW DRAW ONE ON YOUR OWN!

Wind Cave National Park

Wind Cave National Park is home to one of the world's longest and most complex cave systems. It was the first cave system designated as a national park. Portions of the cave are 300 million years old! Wind Cave is known for "boxwork," thin blades of calcite that form a honeycomb pattern on the walls. The Lakota call Wind Cave Maka Oniye, which means "breathing earth." Above ground are prairies full of wildlife, including bison, prairie dogs, and the black-footed ferret, which was once thought to be extinct.

HAVE FUN COLORING THE
WIND CAVE NATIONAL PARK PATCH!

FILL IN THE BLANKS WITH A WORD FROM THE WORD BANK.

1. Wind Cave National Park is located in

   _____.

2. It is the first _____ system to be designated a national park.

3. Wind Cave is particularly known for

   _____.

4. Maka Oniye means "_____ earth."

5. Boxwork forms a _____ pattern.

6. The black-footed ferret was once thought to be _____.

| cave | honeycomb | breathing |
| extinct | South Dakota | boxwork |

Alaska Region

Within the United States, Alaska is the biggest state by land size, is home to the largest national park, and has the longest coastline. It is often referred to as "the land of the midnight sun"; there are times when the sun shines for 24 hours a day in some areas of the state. Alaska's rugged geography encourages activities like fishing, hiking, and wildlife observation. In addition, the mountains and overall landscape hold important environmental and cultural significance. Alaska offers an impressive eight national parks that contain the tallest peak in North America, one of the largest volcanoes in the world, and arctic sand dunes.

Denali National Park & Preserve

Denali National Park & Preserve protects more than six million acres of land and is bigger than the state of New Hampshire. Measuring 20,310 feet, Denali is the tallest peak in North America. Glaciers cover one million acres in the park. Kahiltna Glacier is not only the longest glacier in the park, but it's also the longest glacier in the entire Alaskan Range. Some of Denali's park rangers have four legs; sled dogs help park rangers move around the park. In fact, Denali is the only national park that "employs" sled dogs.

COLOR YOUR OWN SLED DOG! WHAT WILL YOU NAME YOUR SLED DOG?

CAN YOU COMPLETE THIS DENALI NATIONAL PARK & PRESERVE CROSSWORD PUZZLE?

DOWN

1. These cover more than one million acres in the park

3. The longest glacier

ACROSS

2. The state where Denali is located

4. The tallest peak in North America

5. These animals help park rangers

6. Denali National Park is bigger than this state

Gates of the Arctic National Park & Preserve

Gates of the Arctic National Park & Preserve is located above the Arctic Circle and is the northernmost national park. Because there are no roads into the park, visitors must take an air taxi or hike into the park to visit. Anaktuvuk Pass is a small Nunamiut Inupiat village within the park, whose residents have a very long history in the area. Though hiking, camping, and fishing are popular, most visitors come to see the wildlife. Wolverines, caribou, wolves, lynx, musk oxen, and brown bears all live in the park.

MATCH THE NAME OF THE ANIMAL WITH THE CORRECT PICTURE.

WOLVERINE

CARIBOU

WOLF

LYNX

MUSKOX

BROWN BEAR

1. _____

2. _____

3. _____

4. _____

5. _____

6. _____

FIND AND CIRCLE THE WORDS BELOW IN THIS GATES OF THE ARCTIC NATIONAL PARK WORD SEARCH.

```
W  P  R  R  F  Q  X  Y  E  P  Q  O  C  G  U
U  Z  Q  W  Z  O  O  R  L  M  X  G  L  D  L
D  T  C  I  K  E  L  H  C  H  O  N  O  G  A
X  K  J  Y  J  H  P  U  R  H  K  N  J  W  E
H  Y  V  F  T  J  C  Y  I  F  S  C  Z  J  N
A  G  N  I  K  I  H  I  C  A  U  M  H  J  I
V  C  A  R  I  B  O  U  C  S  M  Y  D  B  R
Q  C  Z  D  H  F  E  A  I  R  T  A  X  I  E
L  F  S  F  D  I  T  B  T  H  T  T  D  O  V
S  O  B  E  G  W  E  C  C  F  M  T  S  U  L
H  X  N  Y  L  C  E  L  R  D  N  D  J  L  O
D  N  Z  A  L  A  S  K  A  A  I  Q  Q  B  W
G  S  S  A  P  K  U  V  U  T  K  A  N  A  A
W  R  E  F  I  L  D  L  I  W  X  B  E  Y  B
U  K  K  V  F  N  Y  Z  N  K  W  X  G  D  C
```

ANAKTUVUK PASS   ARCTIC CIRCLE   AIR TAXI

HIKING   LYNX   CARIBOU

ALASKA   MUSK OX

WOLVERINE   WILDLIFE

Glacier Bay National Park & Preserve

Glacier Bay National Park & Preserve contains more than 1,000 tidewater and terrestrial glaciers. The park's most active glacier is Johns Hopkins Glacier, which is about one mile wide, 200 feet deep, and 225 to 300 feet high. Glacier Bay is the sacred homeland of the Huna Tlingit; visitors are welcome in the Huna Ancestors' House to learn about their rich history and culture. Glacier Bay is a humpback whale sanctuary and home to harbor seals and their pups, which can be found on the icebergs and glaciers.

FILL IN THE BLANKS WITH A WORD FROM THE WORD BANK.

1. Glacier Bay National Park & Preserve contains more than _____ glaciers.

2. The park's most active glacier is _____ _____ Glacier.

3. Glacier Bay is the sacred homeland of the _____ _____.

4. Glacier Bay is a _____ _____ sanctuary.

5. Harbor _____ call the icebergs and glaciers home.

Johns Hopkins	1,000	
seals	humpback whale	Huna Tlingit

LEARN HOW TO DRAW A HARBOR SEAL!

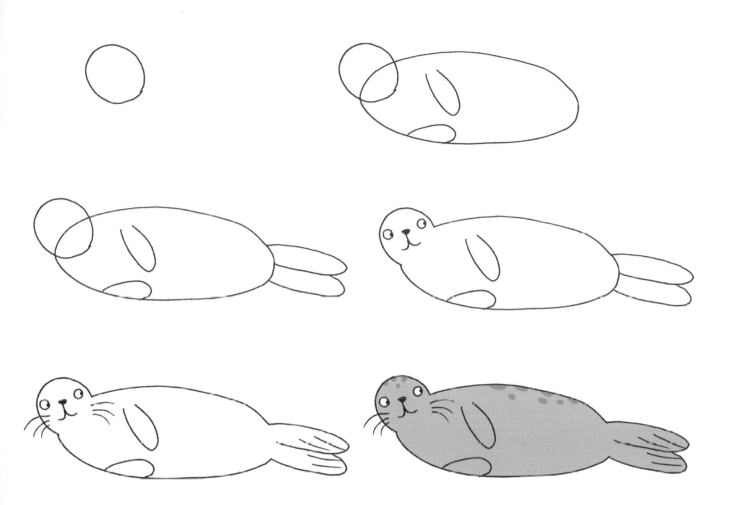

NOW DRAW ONE ON YOUR OWN!

Katmai National Park & Preserve

With over 14 volcanoes, Katmai National Park & Preserve is one of the most active volcanic areas in the world. In June 1912, the largest volcanic eruption of the 20th century occurred within the park. After the Novarupta volcano erupted, thousands of fumaroles (vents on the surface that release hot gases and vapors) filled the area and the Valley of Ten Thousand Smokes was born. The park is famous for brown bears; about 2,000 live in the park.

FILL IN THE MISSING LETTERS.

1. _ a _ m _ i
2. B _ o _ n _ e _ _ s
3. _ r _ p _ io _
4. _ o _ a _ u _ t _
5. _ l _ s _ a
6. V _ l _ _ _ _

YOU CAN MAKE ALMOST 14,000 WORDS OUT OF THE
LETTERS IN KATMAI NATIONAL PARK & PRESERVE.
LIST EIGHT NEW WORDS HERE.

1. _____

2. _____

3. _____

4. _____

5. _____

6. _____

7. _____

8. _____

Kenai Fjords National Park

Located on the Kenai Peninsula, Kenai Fjords National Park works to preserve the Harding Icefield and protect its wildlife. The Harding Icefield covers half the park, and at least 38 glaciers flow from it. The bordering Gulf of Alaska is home to marine life such as harbor seals, orcas, and sea otters. The Sugpiaq (also known as Alutiiq) lived along the Kenai Peninsula for more than 1,000 years, and many of their descendants help interpret artifacts found within the park.

TRACE THE ALUTIIQ WORDS AND START LEARNING A NEW LANGUAGE!

HELLO	CAMA'I
THANK YOU	QUYANAA
BEAR	TAQUKA'AQ
EAGLE	KUM'AGYAK
WHALE	AR'UQ
SEAL	ISUWIQ

CIRCLE THE SIX DIFFERENCES BETWEEN THESE TWO PICTURES OF KENAI FJORDS NATIONAL PARK.

Kobuk Valley National Park

Like Gates of the Arctic, there are no roads into Kobuk Valley National Park; most visitors use an air taxi to enter. The Great Kobuk Sand Dunes in the park are the largest active (unstable and moving) sand dunes in the Arctic. The dunes change as the wind blows the sand around. Kobuk Valley is home to one of the most magnificent migrations in the world: every spring and fall, 250,000 Western Arctic caribou travel through the valley. And every year between June 3 and July 9, the sun doesn't set.

CAN YOU CRACK THE CODE?

The word Kobuk comes from the Inupiat language. Can you use the code to discover what it means?

$\underline{\hphantom{24}}\ \underline{\hphantom{3}}\ \underline{\hphantom{17}}\quad \underline{\hphantom{9}}\ \underline{\hphantom{3}}\ \underline{\hphantom{23}}\ \underline{\hphantom{10}}\ \underline{\hphantom{9}}$
24 3 17   9 3 23 10 9

KEY

1	2	3	4	5	6	7	8	9	10	11	12	13
Q	K	I	D	Y	J	M	A	R	E	N	W	H

14	15	16	17	18	19	20	21	22	23	24	25	26
U	L	O	G	Z	S	C	T	F	V	B	P	X

CAN YOU FIND THE SIX MATCHING PAIRS OF CARIBOU?

Lake Clark National Park & Preserve

Lake Clark National Park & Preserve protects more than four million acres of land, watersheds, wildlife, and two active volcanoes. While Mount Iliamna emits steam regularly, it has never erupted. Mount Redoubt has erupted at least 30 times! The Kvichak watershed produces about 33 percent of the salmon caught in the United States. Lake Clark supports migrating swans resting on their way north and the only known salmon-dependent wolf pack. Bear viewing is popular; visitors may also see caribou, Dall sheep, moose, wolves, and 187 species of birds.

COLOR THE WILDLIFE AND FLOWERS FOUND IN THE PARK.

MATCH THE CLUES ON THE LEFT TO THE CORRECT ANSWERS ON THE RIGHT.

1. This volcano regularly emits steam.

2. This volcano has erupted at least 30 times.

3. This watershed produces lots of salmon.

4. Lake Clark supports these migrating animals.

5. Viewing this large animal is a popular activity.

6. Lake Clark National Park & Preserve protects this number of acres.

A. Four million

B. Swans

C. Bear

D. Mount Iliamna

E. Kvichak

F. Mount Redoubt

Wrangell-St. Elias National Park & Preserve

Wrangell–St. Elias National Park & Preserve is the largest national park. At over 13 million acres, it is the same size as Yosemite National Park, Yellowstone National Park, and the country of Switzerland combined! The Wrangell Volcanic Field consists of thousands of lava flows as well as Mount Wrangell, one of the largest active volcanoes in the world. The park is also home to the largest glacial system in the United States. The Bagley Icefield has multiple glaciers, is six miles wide, 127 miles long, and up to 3,000 feet thick!

CAN YOU UNSCRAMBLE THESE WORDS?

NTOMU ELANWRGL _____

OOLVACN _____

TS LIEAS _____

IIECLDFE _____

LGBYAE _____

ASAKLA _____

COLOR THIS FALL SCENE OF WRANGELL–ST. ELIAS NATIONAL PARK & PRESERVE.

Answer Key

Page 18

People of the Dawnland

Page 21

Page 23

1. West Virginia
2. December
3. Gorge
4. Quarter
5. New River
6. Catwalk

Page 26

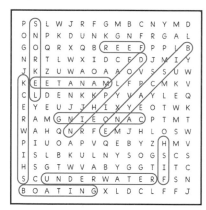

Page 27

Page 29

Page 31

1. False
2. True
3. True
4. False
5. True
6. False
7. True
8. True

Page 32

Rafinesque's big-eared bat

Page 33

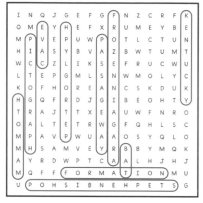

Page 34

1. Congaree
2. South Carolina
3. Forest
4. Boardwalk
5. Firefly
6. Laurel oak

Page 37

1. most
2. 800
3. bear
4. Cades Cove
5. million
6. North Carolina

Page 42

1. Havasupai Tribe
2. Hopi Tribe
3. Hualapai Tribe
4. Kaibab Band of Paiute Indians
5. Las Vegas Band of Paiute Indians
6. Moapa Band of Paiute Indians
7. Navajo Nation
8. Paiute Indian Tribe of Utah
9. Pueblo of Zuni
10. San Juan Southern Paiute Tribe
11. Yavapai-Apache Nation

Page 43

Page 44

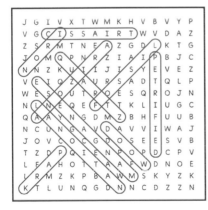

Page 46

1. Saguaro National Park
2. Tucson Mountain District
3. Roadrunner
4. Gila monster
5. Kangaroo rat
6. Diamondback rattlesnake
7. Cactus
8. Arizona

Page 48

1. Colorado
2. Black Canyon
3. Painted Wall
4. Astronomy
5. Cliffs
6. Snowshoe

Page 49

8 bighorn sheep

Page 50

1. E
2. A
3. D
4. C
5. B

Page 53

1. Balcony House
2. Long House
3. Spruce Tree House
4. Step House

Page 54

1. B
2. A
3. C
4. D
5. F
6. E

Page 55

1. Mammals
2. Mountains
3. Colorado
4. Longs Peak
5. Trail Ride Road
6. Continental

Page 56

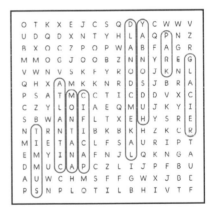

Page 58

1. Desert
2. bucket
3. Lechuguilla Cave
4. 17
5. food
6. 119

Page 59

13 bats

Page 61

1. Gypsum
2. White Sands
3. Fossil
4. Footprint
5. Columbian mammoth
6. Dire wolf
7. New Mexico

Page 64

1. Salt Basin Dunes
2. Guadalupe
3. Top of Texas
4. Guadalupe Peak
5. Fossil Reef

Page 65

1. C
2. A
3. B
4. D
5. E

Page 67

1. D
2. C
3. A
4. B

Page 68

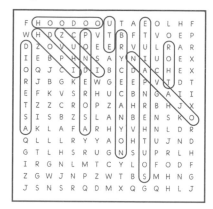

Page 69

Page 70

1. False
2. True
3. True
4. False
5. True

Page 71

1. Horseshoe Canyon
2. Maze
3. Needles
4. Utah
5. Colorado
6. Island in the Sky

Page 72

1. Settlers
2. Natural bridge
3. Wrinkle
4. Waterpocket Fold
5. Monocline
6. Utah
7. Capitol Reef

Page 74

Mukuntuweap National Monument

Page 75

Page 77

1. Wyoming
2. Airport
3. Glacier
4. Grand Teton
5. Coyote
6. Bison
7. Eagle

Page 78

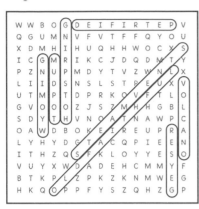

Page 85

1. Santa Rosa
2. Pacific
3. San Miguel
4. Santa Barbara
5. Anacapa
6. Santa Cruz
7. Island scrub jay
8. California

Page 86

1. Badwater Basin
2. Artists Palette
3. hottest
4. 134 degrees
5. ghost towns
6. California

Page 87

Page 89

1. True
2. False
3. True
4. False
5. True
6. False

Page 91

1. D
2. A
3. C
4. F
5. B
6. E

Page 92

Snow Mountain

Page 96

1. Del Norte Coast
2. Prairie Creek
3. Jedediah Smith
4. Hyperion
5. Crescent Beach
6. Pacific Ocean
7. Roosevelt elk

Page 97

Tree A: 5 years

Tree B: 8 years

Tree C: 13 years

Page 98

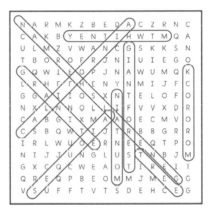

Page 101

Buffalo Soldiers

Page 102

1. volcano
2. sun
3. bamboo
4. silversword
5. Summit
6. Hawaii

Page 104

1. Volcanoes
2. Hawaii
3. Kilauea
4. Mauna Loa
5. Crater
6. Pacific Ocean

Page 105

Page 107

1. Wasatch
2. bristlecone
3. Prometheus
4. glacier
5. Lehman Caves
6. Fremont

Page 108

1. Volcano
2. Wizard Island
3. Volcanic cone
4. Lake
5. Mazama newt
6. Oregon
7. Collapsed

Page 112

1. False
2. True
3. True
4. False
5. True
6. False

Page 113

1. Wolverine
2. Lynx
3. Pika
4. River otter
5. Grizzly bear
6. Wolf

Page 114

1. Hoh Rain Forest
2. Lake Crescent
3. Mountain
4. Beaches
5. Starfish
6. Gray whale
7. Washington

Page 115

17 Olympic marmots

Page 119

1. Quapaw
2. Buckstaff

Page 121

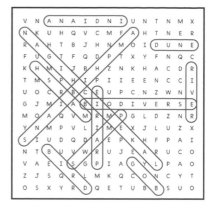

Page 123

1. Michigan
2. Mammals
3. Gray wolf
4. Winter
5. Boat
6. Superior
7. Islands

Page 125

1. Voyageurs
2. Minnesota
3. Travelers
4. Sand Point
5. Rainy Lake
6. Fish
7. Lights
8. Aurora borealis

Page 128

1. D
2. A
3. E
4. B
5. C

Page 130

1. Ohio
2. Cuyahoga Valley
3. Railroad
4. Brandywine Falls
5. Ledges Overlook
6. Crooked River

Page 132

Pronghorn

Page 135

1. South Dakota
2. cave
3. boxwork
4. breathing
5. honeycomb
6. extinct

Page 139

1. Glaciers
2. Alaska
3. Kahiltna
4. Denali
5. Sled dogs
6. New Hampshire

Page 140

1. Caribou
2. Brown bear
3. Wolf
4. Lynx
5. Muskox
6. Wolverine

Page 141

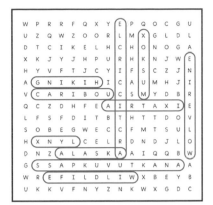

Page 142

1. 1,000
2. Johns Hopkins
3. Huna Tlingit
4. humpback whale
5. seals

Page 144

1. Katmai
2. Brown bears
3. Eruption
4. Novarupta
5. Alaska
6. Valley

Page 147

Page 148

Big River

Page 151

1. D
2. F
3. E
4. B
5. C
6. A

Page 152

1. Mount Wrangell
2. Volcano
3. St. Elias
4. Icefield
5. Bagley
6. Alaska

About the Author

NICOLE CLAESEN has always loved traveling, especially with her husband and two sons. They visit as many national parks as possible. After several years of traveling with her family, she wanted to share their adventures, trip itinerary suggestions, and lessons learned, and that's when her website and blog, Suitcase and a Map (suitcaseandamap.com), was born. It lets her write about family travel and share the magic of seeing the world through the eyes of children. She is the author of *Fun with 50 States* and is now excited to share the national parks with you!

About the Artist

CANDELA FERRÁNDEZ is a freelance illustrator based in Barcelona, Spain. After studying fine arts at Salamanca University, she earned a postgraduate degree in illustration at EINA (Barcelona). When she was a child, she loved looking for bugs and little animals around gardens. Now she draws them. Children, flowers, plants, and animals define her personal universe, which she also expresses in ceramic pieces. Her illustrations have been published by, among others, Milan Presse, Éditions Larousse, Fleurus, and Penguin Random House, including those in *Fun with 50 States*. Visit Candela online at candelaferrandez.com.